Shantti,

Thanks for being an encouragement to all you encounter. May God continue to use your hearts + talents for His glory.

—Sarah

Published by CreateSpace.

Cover design: Carly Wilkie with iCandy Graphics & Web Design.

Geezer. Punk. Whatever. A Practical Guide to Bridging the Generational Gap. / Sarah J. Gibson

ISBN: 0-6927-1566-5

Contents

Preface

Okay, you get it. There are differences between the generations, and these differences can have a profound effect on how we work together, communicate, and resolve conflict.

What You Will Find

This guide contains quick, easy-to-use information about the generations that you can use to identify bottom line next steps for application on the job—and in your life. I wrote the book to help you answer these questions:

- What do I need to know about the generations, in general?

- Why are generational differences important?

- What specific points should I know about the generations to make working together work better?

- Now what?

If you have limited knowledge of generational differences, you will walk away knowing more about the characteristics and tendencies of each generation. If you come to this book with more understanding of the subject, you will learn how to apply your current knowledge to your work situation. Either way, you will find this guide's key points about the four current working generations helpful in strengthening inter-generational communication.

How To Use This Book

As you read, watch for these icons indicating helpful explanations and application questions:

 "Common Questions" sections highlight what folks most often ask about a particular topic.

 "Talk to Me" anecdotes provide real-life perspectives on a particular topic.

 "Tools for Real Life" sections give you an opportunity to consider how you might apply what you've learned in real life.

If you're new to the topic of generational differences, be sure to read the short descriptions before each chart as well as "Common Questions" sections. If you're more familiar with generational fundamentals, you may wish to check out the extended chart pages to compare your perceptions to generational trends, then turn to "What Now" sections for specific examples that may be useful.

Overview of the Contents

This book is divided into three main sections:

- Chapter 1 presents the fundamentals of the generations, including the birth years that define them, the defining events that shaped them, and the shared characteristics we've come to expect as a result.

- Chapter 2 covers each of the generations at work—why we work, what's important to us at work, our unique workplace contributions and challenges, why we consider changing jobs, and what you can expect in our resumes and job searches. Here we also zoom in on putting generational communication styles to use.

- In Chapter 3 you will find very specific, practical information for managers and teams. Here you'll find out about the generations' management styles, how we see team members and coworkers, feedback preferences, motivators and de-motivators, and beliefs about training and education. Here we also zoom in on how best to support the generations through conflict and change.

The book ends with a list of additional resources for those interested in learning more about the generations.

Beyond These Pages

You will not find here a recounting of the history and research behind what we know about generational differences. Others have done an excellent job of documenting this important information. The Resources section at the end of this book lists books and websites I recommend for people with limited time who want to know more about this topic's main ideas and points.

This book is intended to be one tool in your communication toolbox. What you learn from this guide and its generational perspective is just one piece of a bigger puzzle. I recommend combining what you find here with other communication tools as you assemble a comprehensive picture of your coworkers, staff and family to enhance communication and productivity.

Acknowledgements

This book is the product of years of experience and a passion for helping others succeed at their jobs. Learning and teaching about generational differences has impacted my career, pointing me in new directions I didn't know were even an option.

To all of you who have helped me succeed through this time—my encouragers, editors, and content contributors—thank you!

Susan Bassett	Lynne Lancaster	Amy Olejniczak
Darren Boyer	Michael Leitz	A.B. Orlik
Tracy Bredeson	Debra Niehaus	Eric Peterson
Carol Bracewell	Nan Pum	Beth Sherven
Paul Cooke	Anne Mancl	DeLaina Siltman
Denise Elmer	Christine Melland	

To one of my greatest encouragers, the man who said, "Sarah, set a deadline. Write it. Get moving," I offer special thanks. Herb Delehanty, you rock!

To my immediate family, thank you. Don, you've been patient, encouraging and more than I deserve. Grace and Kyle, this book is being published with the hope that you, too, will see the optimism of our times.

Without the three of you, I would never leave my office. Thanks for giving me a reason to come home.

The Author

Sarah Gibson is President of Accent Learning and Consulting, LLC, a learning development and consulting firm she founded in 2004 in Madison, Wisconsin.

Through keynote presentations, consulting, coaching, and teaching, Sarah has worked with a variety of employees and executives on topics ranging from generational communication, business writing, communication styles and presentation skills.

Sarah has worked with companies across the US and Canada and brings her expertise to improve organizational culture and communication.

Prior to starting her own business, Sarah facilitated training and development in corporate settings. In addition to her corporate work, Sarah taught public relations, media writing and public speaking at the University of Wisconsin–Whitewater and North Dakota State University. She has a Master's degree in communication from North Dakota State University and continues her work as an adjunct instructor for local colleges.

And to give Gen Xers and Millennials the bio information they really want: Sarah has an amazing spouse and two delightful children. She strives to balance her love of work with family and enjoys the challenge of both immensely. During the summer, she and her family spend as much time as they can on their boat cruising lakes near Madison, Wisconsin.

CHAPTER ONE

Zooming Out
for the Fundamentals

Identifying a Generation by Birth Years

Generational trends are identified by demographers, and even they don't agree on how to name the generations or which years define them. For this book, and in my workshops, I use the start and end years offered by Neil Howe and William Strauss in their book, *Generations: The History of America's Future, 1584–2069*, and the common names of the generations used by Howe and Strauss and Lynne Lancaster and David Stillman, authors of *When Generations Collide*. (I recommend both in the Resource section.)

So, for our purposes:

- The World War II (WWII) generation—also known as the Loyalists, Silent Generation, or Traditionalists—spans birth years 1925 to 1945.

- The Baby Boomers—also known as the Beat Generation, Hippies, or Yuppies—were born between 1946 and 1964.

- Generation X (GenX)—sometimes called the 13th Generation or Slackers—spans birth years 1965 to 1981.

- Members of the Millennial generation were born between 1982 and 2000. You may see this generation referred to as Adapters, the Echo-Boom, the Entitled Generation, Gen Y, Gen Why, or Gen Text.

COMMON QUESTION: *Does it matter that one person says the Baby Boom generation starts in 1960 and another says 1964—or any other generation's start and end date, for that matter?*

ANSWER: *No. What's interesting for our purposes are the trends that stem from experiences of the generation's time period as a whole. Read on to hear why.*

The Role of Defining Events

To explain generational differences in character, preferences, and behaviors, demographers look beyond birth years to childhood experiences called defining events—events that complete this statement: "During my childhood, I remember where I was when…"

A defining event happens before we are 18 years old and has the potential to shape our generation. While a defining event may be a major worldwide event, major worldwide events are only defining events for some of us experiencing them—those who are younger than 18 at the time.

For example, I can say, "I remember where I was when 9/11 happened." However, since I was in my mid-20s, that event impacted my generation less than the generation of someone under the age of 18. The young people who were under 18 at the of 9/11 have had their generational perspective of safety altered more dramatically than those of us who were adults when this happened.

The Result: Shared Characteristics

For each generation, the defining events we experience shape the trends or characteristics of our generation. Think of it this way. When someone asks us to picture the American flag, most of us visualize red and white stripes and white stars on a blue corner piece. Arguably, we can assume most of the people we interact with have a matching visual image.

For many of us, the same is true of generational characteristics. There are some characteristics that most of us agree represent a generation. Does that mean everyone thinks the same thing about either the flag or the generations? No. However, the trends are marked by the common experiences of many.

How this works

The defining events that occurred before we were 18 years old shape our generational characteristics. For example:

- The Great Depression of the 1930s birthed an entire generation of frugal savers who recycle and reuse everything possible.

- The birth of 80 million babies during the Baby Boom created a generation of competitive, driven achievers.

- Dual-income families shaped a generation of latch-key kids (Gen X) who still function independently of anyone or anything.

- School shootings and terrorism prompted a generation of globally centered young people concerned with personal safety.

Table 1 on page 6 is a quick snapshot of the generations, their defining events, and a list of characteristics that stem from those events.

Table 1: Snapshot of Four Generations in the Workplace

	WORLD WAR II	BABY BOOM
Approximate birth years	• 1925 to 1945	• 1946 to 1964
Population	• 52 million	• 80 million
Also known as...	• Loyalists • Silent Generation • Traditionalists	• Beat Generation • Hippies • Yuppies
Key defining events	• Radio • World War II • Atomic bomb • GI Bill • Stock market crash • Great Depression • Korean War	• Assassinations of John F. Kennedy, Robert Kennedy, Martin Luther King Jr. • Civil rights • Cold War • Vietnam • Sex, drugs, rock'n'roll • Television • Women's liberation
Generational profile	• Duty rules conscience • Do what's right no matter the cost to me • Follow orders, no questions • Loyal, hard-working • Military-style leadership • Patriotic	• Competitive • Status driven • Optimistic • Rebellious

GENERATION X	MILLENNIAL
• 1965 to 1981	• 1982 to 2000
• 46 million	• 76 million
• Gen X • 13th Generation • Slackers	• Adapters • Echo-Boom • Entitled Generation • Gen Y
• Watergate • Challenger explosion • AIDS • Cable television and MTV • Single-parent homes • Latch-key kids • Milk cartons with missing kids • Personal computers at home • Internet (www) begins	• 9/11 • Smart phones • Columbine and other school shootings • Fall of the Berlin Wall • War in Iraq • Hurricane Katrina • Tsunami aid • iPods, YouTube, Facebook • 2008 Obama election • 2009 economic downturn
• American dream of perfect family/home/job not realistic • Independent • Self-preservation is key • Skeptical	• Creative • Fast-paced multi-taskers • Always connected to the collective whole • Globally connected and focused • Optimistic • Patriotic • Street smart

COMMON QUESTION: *Why the magic age of 18?*

ANSWER: *The idea of formative years is attributed to Morris Massey who stated, "Where you were is what you are." In the 1960s, Massey claimed that our most formative age is around 10 years old. Most generational researchers expand this formative window to include your earliest conscious memories (around age five or so) and continue until age 18.*

What about Individual Differences?

Exceptions to these generational trends abound. You may be the exception. There are several things affecting how strongly we match our generational profile.

- Your birth year. Because generation dates aren't set in stone, you may be what experts call a "cusper" or "tweener"—a person born within 2–3 years of a generation's start or end date. You may find yourself possessing characteristics of both generations.

- Your sphere of influence growing up. For example, I'm an Xer with high Baby Boomer traits because all of my siblings are mid-generation Boomers.

- Your birthplace. First-generation Americans, regardless of their birth year, tend to have characteristics similar to the WWII generation. As their children become influenced by American culture, these children have characteristics more typical of their birth generation.

- Your culture. The characteristics of the generations in other cultures differ from those here in the U.S., when you look at older generations (Baby Boomer and World War II). Interestingly, studies suggest generational dif-ferences are much less signifi-cant in Gen X and Millennial generations across the globe when you look at industrialized nations. A Millennial in India has simi-lar generational traits as a Millennial in Europe or the U.S. Why is this? Many of our workplaces are global enterprises that require cross-cultural communication. It's logical the more global we become, the more experiences (defining events) we share in common with other countries. And, just as we individually bring unique experiences to our work, individuals from different cul-tures will continue to bring his or her own unique cultural experi-ence to the communication process.

- Your baggage. Each of us has unique circumstances and experi-ences that have shaped us. I use "baggage" to refer to the whole collection of experiences you're carrying around from your past. This may have a profound influence on your outlook, some of which may match your generation—or not. For example, if you lost a parent as a child and had to provide for your family at the age of 14, you likely don't have the same perspective as someone with a carefree childhood.

Generational Characteristic or a Natural Stage of Life?

COMMON QUESTION: *Are GenXers really lazy, or is this just something we all go through as we mature and get older?*

ANSWER: *Gen Xers as a generation were labeled "lazy" when they were young (and now we say the same of Mil-lennials). Now that many Xers are in their 30s and early 40s, they've become entrenched in their careers as a means of providing for their families. But none of us wanted to put in long hours or do nasty jobs when we were 18, so this lazi-ness isn't a generational issue, it's a maturation stage. We'll see the same transition happen as Millennials mature.*

We all go through certain maturity points, and these are different than generational characteristics. When we are 18, for example, most of us think our parents are the dumbest people on Earth. (Sorry, mom and dad!) As we get older, we see the wisdom our parents have offered us, and we grow to appreciate them more.

While each generation hits the same life stages or maturation points, we each bring our unique generational perspective to that time in our lives. Look at how two generations handled the childbearing life stage:

- When Boomers started having children, both parents often worked. Boomer women proved their capabilities and channeled their driven nature into securing women's rights in the working world.

- When GenXers started having children, they took their passion for work-life balance and fought to work on their own terms, including flex-time and telecommuting.

Each generation faced the life stage from its own perspective, so the traits of their generation showed up in their reaction to the particular life stage.

CHAPTER TWO

Zooming In on the Generations at Work

A Closer Look

In Chapter One we summarized the different styles and preferences of each generation. In Chapter Two we answer, "What now?" by sharing information you can apply today as you interact with each generation. Later, in Chapter Three, we provide additional information to support managers and intergenerational teams.

Before going on, check out Table 2 on the next few pages. There you'll find details about each generation's expectations in the workplace, including:

- Why we work

- What's important to us at work

- Our unique workplace contributions and challenges

- Why we consider changing jobs

- What you can expect in our resumes and job searches

We'll use information from Table 2 throughout this chapter. Take some time to honestly evaluate the "Tools for Real Life" sections, too, to see what you're doing well and what you could improve in your communication encounters.

Table 2: The Generations at Work

	WORLD WAR II	BABY BOOM
Approx. birth years	• 1925 to 1945	• 1946 to 1964
Why work?	• Duty—it's how I provide for my family	• Self-fulfillment—I want to make a difference
Work ethic	• Dedicated and loyal	• Driven and committed
Workplace contributions	• Loyal • Hard-working • Consistent • Gets the job done, no matter the cost • Has extended experience and corporate history	• Driven • Dedicated • Competitive • Excellent team player • Drives team to best competitive output • Has corporate experience and history • Values research and well-made products and services • Goes above and beyond
Workplace challenges	• Dislikes change • Won't buck system • Dislikes and withdraws from conflict	• Big on ideas • Process more important than outcome • Sensitive to critique from younger workers
Work in context	• Give my all to the company because the company rewards loyalty	• Work to prove myself and get ahead financially
Work-life balance	• Want support as I shift balance during retirement	• Want support to balance aging parents and adult children's needs

Geezer. Punk. Whatever.

GENERATION X	MILLENNIAL
• 1965 to 1981	• 1982 to 2000
• To pay the bills—this is a job, not my life	• To grow my skill set and help others
• Balanced work and home life	• Enthusiastic and prepared to jump
• Adaptable • Creative • Independent self-starter • Not intimidated by authority • Plays devil's advocate and asks, "Why are we doing this?" • Values work-life balance • Technically savvy	• Creative • Collaborative • Multi-talented • Multi-tasking • Capable in fast-paced environment • Technically savvy • Highly diverse • Looks for wellness of all on team • Loves fun
• Impatient • Not politically savvy in the corporate world • Cynical • Dislikes unnecessary relationship tending and schmoozing	• High, unrealistic expectations (including starting at the top) • Dislikes conflict • Lack of real-world experience
• Protect home life by working hard, then going home	• Believe I make a significant impact when heard and respected
• Want balance now, not when I retire	• Want flexibility to balance all activities

• Continued on next page…

Geezer. Punk. Whatever.

Table 2: The Generations at Work

	WORLD WAR II	BABY BOOM
Ideal career	• One job	• A couple of jobs, but all changes made with purpose
Why change jobs?	• I wouldn't—at least not without good reason	• Because there's a chance to improve a situation or if there's a specific reason to
Resume is...	• A handshake	• A list of accomplishments
Job search style	• Why would I look for a new job?	• Why would I tell anyone I'm looking for a new job?

Generational Myopia: Taking the Blinders Off

Myopia is a type of nearsightedness. For our purposes, myopia means we see what we want to about ourselves. Generational myopia refers to when we see only our own generational perspectives and not the perspectives of other generations.

When people in my sessions have a lot of fun, participants joke about how their generation is the best looking, most fun and best ever. Now, they're kidding around, but we all tend think that about our generation—to some degree.

When we acknowledge our generational myopia, we can see the bigger picture and the contributions each generation makes to the whole. Sometimes that requires us giving up some of our own preferences to meet the needs of others.

In order to experience the richness of our environments at work and beyond, we need to remember that other generations have differing perspectives that can benefit our worlds too, if we're willing to look.

Geezer. Punk. Whatever.

GENERATION X	MILLENNIAL
• Several jobs, some as long as 4-5 years	• Many jobs, all used to further and explore who I am
• Because I want more flexibility and control	• Because I want new skills
• The way to get an interview	• An online formality
• Why would anyone care if I'm looking for a new job	• Why wouldn't I be looking for a new job?

TALK TO ME: *Three years ago, I found myself teaming with a World War II/Boomer cusper (see page 6) to promote a communication event aimed at employees of all ages. When writing promotional language for the program, my colleague consistently wrote things like, "give you a competitive edge," "make you more money," and "give you connections." From my Xer perspective, I was using phrases like "will make your networking more efficient" and "give you more credibility with customers." After some frustration, we talked about why we wanted to use the phrases we did, and ultimately we blended our perspectives for a better product that neither of us could have achieved individually.*

TOOLS FOR REAL LIFE: *When you collaborate with your multi-generational team, what are you doing well? Where is your generational myopia blinding you?*

Common Wish List, Different Definitions

Working with multiple generations isn't necessarily easy, but recognizing where we share common ground can be tremendously helpful. As much as all generations are different, all generations are the same, too. In reality, we all want the same things from our jobs. For example, each generation wants:

- An enjoyable job

- Fulfillment and purpose

- Good benefits and pay

- Perspective on what's important

- Respect

- Stability in the company and job

- Validation and appreciation

So if we all want the same thing, what's the big deal about generations? The trick is that each generation defines certain terms differently. For example, a World War II person shows respect to everyone, but especially to those who are above him in the chain of command. An Xer respects people who prove themselves competent, and may not respect an elder, or someone higher in the chain of command, who hasn't done that yet.

Taming the Clash of Expectations

Because we all want the same thing, but go about defining each of the things we want differently, we end up with a clash of expectations.

When it feels like communication isn't going how you'd envisioned, consider these questions to look at the big picture:

- What is the underlying concern here?

- Is this a negotiable item, or is It one of my non-negotiable items? Is it something I can or should change?

- What are the expectations of each participant?

- What is a win situation for each participant?

- How might a win-win be possible?

- What would that look like?

- How can I communicate the outcome in a way that each generation hears what is being said?

 COMMON QUESTION: *One of the most common generational clashes I see is over work-life balance. So the question is: Why is Gen X so intensely focused on work-life balance?*

ANSWER: *Xers were very independent youngsters. Many of their families were the first to have two working parents, leaving the kids to fend for themselves. Because of this, Xers tend to want to protect their families from the separation and loss they felt as children. They will run away from extracurricular work activities—even agree to work after their kiddos go to bed—if it means going home to watch their kids' soccer games or see their little ones before bed. They work hard to preserve their family units, and they fiercely protect their time to do that.*

Millennials, on the other hand, grew up in a world where technology makes many things possible, including working from home or at a job that didn't exist 5 years ago. Millennials believe that they will make the biggest impact if they have healthy balance in both their home and work lives. After all, that's what their Boomer parents said they should strive for. Now, we watch as Millennials brin that perspective to the workplace.

TOOLS FOR REAL LIFE: *Consider which generational perspectives are most/least represented among your leadership team(s). What impact might that have in your organization?*

Take a look at your human resource policies or employee handbook. In what ways are different generations' expectations reflected? Where can you see room for improvement?

Impact of the Millennials

I get a lot of questions about Millennials, because they're the most recent generation to join the workplace. One question I hear often: Won't Millennials just merge into business culture like the Xers did? Is this a big deal?

Before I talk about Millennials, I want us to think about Baby Boomers entering the workplace. Boomers stepped into a WWII organization and said things like, "Why can't a woman have that job?" or "Can't we be just as productive if we wear business casual?"

The changes the 80 million Boomers brought to the workplace were as shattering to the WWII generation as the changes Millennials hope to bring to today's workplace.

To answer the question, "Won't Millennials just merge into existing business culture like previous generations?" the answer is: yes, *and*. Yes, Millennials will merge into existing business culture *and* they will bring their own twist to business norms.

One difference between Xers and Millennials is the sheer numbers of the Millennial generation (76 million). Xers have only 40 million in their generation, so they simply didn't have the numbers needed to institute the changes a larger generation can.

Because of the large numbers of Millennials, our workplaces may need to adapt more. When the 40 million Xers entered the workplace, there weren't many jobs. They lived with the jobs they could get (happy or not). Seventy-six million Millennials are entering the workforce at a time when 80 million Baby Boomers are leaving. They are entering a marketplace where we need them as employees. They have more of an upper hand than the prior generation, so yes, they will merge into our busi-ness culture, and they will make some demands about flex-ibility and working on their terms.

I recommend that companies identify non-negotiables, things about their work cultures that are part of the core of their business regardless of what generation works there, and get creative from there. If a suit and tie are required attire and that's the business' non-negotiable, that's fine. However, businesses can't expect to avoid adapting to any new changes in the coming years.

COMMON QUESTION: *Millennials are a juxtaposition of group orientation and individual isolation. How does that work?*

ANSWER: *Millennials have been taught that even one of them can make a difference. Just look at those who have started their own charities on Facebook and in their communities. In contrast to Xers, who, when they saw negative things going on in their world chose to cocoon and watch out for themselves and their families, Millennials think, "Wow, I can do anything I want. But think what I can do if I had a whole series of me's working together!" They see the power of powerful teams, but they connect with their teams differently than previous generations. When Millennials walk the mall in a group, they are in a group, but each is talking with a different person on her/his cell phone. Individuals connected to a group, connected to other individuals. It's an interesting twist.*

Intentionally Connecting and Communicating

Each of us has preferences when it comes to communication styles and approaches—and which generation we belong to has something to do with that. It's helpful to recognize that what may seem natural to us might not be natural to other generations. Not that there's anything wrong with our approach (or theirs), it's just that our communication may miss the mark—or even be perceived as offensive.

To smooth out some of the bumpy spots in communication, try listening with a twist: Pay particular attention to key words and strategies associated with each generation. See Table 3 for ideas.

With the information from Table 3 in your toolbox, you may find it easier to understand and be understood by other generations.

 TOOLS FOR REAL LIFE: *Brutally honest communication*

Millennials have an interesting mix of brutal honesty with others and a lacking ability to fail.

This plays out when you ask a Millennial for feedback. Most often they will tell you exactly what went wrong or how the process sucked.

On the flipside, when you need to bring con-structive feedback to a Millennial, it can crush him or her if not handled carefully.

This contrast drives many managers and co-workers crazy. How can Millennials be brutally honest to you, but not take any feedback in return?

The answer lies in two pieces of the Millennials' defining events. Their honesty comes from Boomer parents who encouraged their children to talk about anything with them. And not only did they encourage the Millennials to discuss things, the Millen-nials were often treated as equals to their parents. The result, a young person with an expectation that his/her opinion was as valuable as an older member of the family.

Continued on page 26

Table 3: Effective Communication Across the Generations

	WORLD WAR II	BABY BOOM
Approximate birth years	• 1925 to 1945	• 1946 to 1964
Strategies that work	• Focus on words rather than body language • Give them time to process their thoughts before asking opinions • Expect them not to question or challenge authority or the status quo publicly • Limit how much private information you share • Show politeness, use very traditional etiquette (using Mr. and Mrs., for example) • Use inclusive language (we, us) • Use face-to-face or written communication	• Answer questions thoroughly and expect to be pressed for details • Remember Boomers are the "show me" generation, so watch your body language • Speak openly and directly, but avoid controlling language • Use face-to-face or telephone the first time, then follow up with electronic communication
Hot buttons to avoid	• Don't leave them feeling as if they don't matter any more • Don't flash the new, improved version of their work in front of them while mentioning how you came up with a better product in seconds	• Don't leave them feeling old and obsolete • Don't move forward without getting their take on the situation
Instead try...	• Acknowledge their experience • Demonstrate your respect for what they respect—having put in their time, working their way up, going to the school of hard knocks • Mention how you couldn't have done what you did without their ground work	• Gain their support through consensus and participation • Recognize and thank them for their accomplishments • Use their knowledge of past projects to learn

GENERATION X	MILLENNIAL
• 1965 to 1981	• 1981 to 2000
• Be transparent and say what you mean • Expect open communication regardless of position, title or tenure • Talk in bullet points • Ask them for and provide them with regular feedback and information • Use an informal communication style • Use email as a primary communication tool	• Learn their language and speak it (but don't try to sound cool) • Talk in short sound bytes • Use an informal communication style • Eliminate paper and think eco-friendly • Communicate through technology (IM, texting) • Respond quickly to emails and text messages • Use real-time access to information that is updated and fresh
• Don't ask them to attend things for the sake of corporate politics • Don't insist on meeting at a time they've clearly cordoned off as family time	• Don't call them "kiddo" • Don't tell them to wait for reality to teach them
• Lay out why something is necessary • Expect them to be skeptical and unimpressed • Offer flexible options and gracious ways of saying no • Be genuinely interested in them and their lives • Offer them tasks they can do independently before reporting back to the team	• Channel their energies into difficult processes that require new ideas • Expect they can do way more than you think and plan accordingly • Protect them from miserable failure—correct at easy-to-fix points until they learn the ropes • Provide practical advice about people and corporate politics/culture • Set up give-and-take mentoring relationships—Millennials have much to teach other generations

The second piece, the lessened ability to take in criticism, lies again, in parenting styles. Boomer parents often coached their children through scenarios, not allowing them to fail, but instead correcting the Millennials' actions before failure occurred. The workplace impact is that Millennials don't want to fail, and many believe they can't fail and are crushed when it happens the first time. Many managers report losing Millennials after the Millennial failed at a project, not because failure was unacceptable in the company out-side the manager's expectations, but because the Millennial couldn't face the failure.

My advice to businesses and an additional tool for real life: create an environment that allows and teaches Millennials how to fail safely and then shows the benefits of failing and retrying.

Zooming In
for Teams and Managers

Bringing Out the Best in the Generations

In Chapters One and Two you learned (or reviewed) about the generations, particularly about their unique workplace expectations, preferences, strengths and challenges. In Chapter Three we bring together information specifically to support managers and teams working across generations.

Why do Xers struggle with managing Baby Boomers? Why do Boomers struggle to manage Millennials? It's all a matter of perspective. And while it's implicitly woven throughout this book, it's worth mentioning here that we tend to manage according to our preferred style, which is affected by our generational perspective. It is as important to be aware of generational differences in management and team leadership as it is in more general communication.

 TALK TO ME: *On my team of employees, I have a series of Gen Xers who are used to being thrown to the wolves when I send a project their direction. The Xers fight, snarl and sort their way through the material until they think they know what I want done. I don't even think twice about letting them scramble. I think they expect and enjoy that.*

When I added a couple of Boomers to my team, I found that I needed to invest more time up front to make a Boomer comfortable with a project and the project's success. This often entailed face-to-face meetings.

In addition, my Monday morning email blast to the Xers had worked beautifully for years, but one Boomer asked specifically that I call weekly just to touch base. It mattered to her that I knew she was working, even though all I cared about was that the work got done. The other Boomer didn't ask for the update by phone; she simply called rather than responding to my emails.

For managers and teams wanting to understand the generations better from this point of view, we created Table 4 on page 32. It includes detailed information about:

- Management styles

- How we see team members and coworkers

- Feedback preferences (how often, what form, phrases that click)

- Motivators and de-motivators

- Beliefs about training and education

 COMMON QUESTION: *What does it mean that Baby Boomers have a "change of command" management style? Where did this come from?*

ANSWER: *Think back to their growing up years. As a generation, Boomers questioned authority and took on established social norms such as segregation and women's rights. As a result, their generation looks at authority as either positive (I love this) or bad (I hate this and have to do something about it). Often if a Boomer dislikes the authority over him or her, he or she will work to change the situation—by offering to help, vying for a new position in the company, or finding a new spot to land. Awareness of this tendency can be useful both for Boomer managers and for those who lead or manage them.*

TOOLS FOR REAL LIFE: *Think about how you manage. Does your style reflect your generation, or do you adapt to the preferences of other generations?*

Generational Motivators and De-motivators

Regardless of our age or job title, we all want to be acknowledged for our contributions to the workplace. But how we prioritize what motivates us varies across generations.

Specific examples of motivators and de-motivators for each of the generations appear in Table 4 on page 32. Understanding these preferences can make the difference between a reward that leaves your employee bouncing down the hall and one that leaves her wondering "Um…thanks, I think."

TALK TO ME: *Here's a classic example of a reward that went underappreciated. After speaking at a highly prestigious meeting of executives in our region, I was presented with a beautiful silver-plated pen with my name inscribed on it. Graciously, I said thank you—and I do think it's a beautiful pen. When I got home, I called my sister, a Boomer, and told her about this beautiful-but-fairly-impractical gift. She laughed and said, "Sarah, this is a generation gap. You've reached the epitome of Boomer status. You got a pen with your name on it!" Lesson learned: We each reward from our generation's preferences, and it's worth paying attention to the receiver's preferences, too.*

Table 4: More Information for Teams and Managers

	WORLD WAR II	BABY BOOM
Approximate birth years	• 1925 to 1945	• 1946 to 1964
Comfortable management style	• Chain of command	• Change of command
Team and coworkers are	• Part of the chain	• Competition
Feedback that works	• No news is good news—feedback indicates I did something wrong	• Occasional written/ documented feedback
Phrases that click	• Your experience is respected here • We value your knowledge and perseverance	• Without your dedication, I'm not sure what we would have done • You are important to our success • We need you
Motivators	• Delayed reward • Practical, real-world information • My sense of duty • Because it's the right thing to do	• Acknowledgement of my contributions • Challenge and competition (carrots and sticks) • Challenge and new opportunities to show my talent • Money • Prestige, reputation
De-motivators	• Not feeling valued or appreciated for history/ experience	• Lack of appreciation, respect, and recognition
Beliefs about training and education	• Learn it on your own, I did (school of hard knocks)	• With too much training, the employees will leave, but personally I value education/ training

Geezer. Punk. Whatever.

GENERATION X	MILLENNIAL
• 1965 to 1981	• 1981 to 2000
• Self-command, independent	• No command, collaborate
• Independent partners	• Essential key to the team
• Immediate and ongoing, usually face-to-face	• Instantaneous feedback at the push of a button
• You can do it however you want • We keep up on technology • We're family friendly • Our work world is flexible • How can we help you?	• You'll be working with other creative people • We encourage community and volunteer activities • You can make a difference here
• Flexibility in hours and work options (telecommuting, alternate hours, daycare on site, healthy lives programs) • Immediate feedback (not in 6 months) • Independence, self-control • Practical things that can be earned and used immediately • Time off • Transparency from leadership	• Company with a conscience • Flexibility in work options (including where to work) • Work friendships , from CEO to peers • Fun environments • People who listen to my ideas and don't dismiss them immediately • Praise • Immediate career paths • Big projects that grow my skills
• Lack of intellectual stimulation • Lack of work-life balance	• One-dimensional work • Lack of challenge
• There's never enough training—more is better; if you don't train them enough, employees might leave	• The only constant is change, so training will be continuous

Geezer. Punk. Whatever.

TOOLS FOR REAL LIFE: *Think about how you motivate your employees or potential employees. Do you sell your company, programs, and jobs using things that would motivate your generation or theirs?*

What additional motivators could you incorporate to reach each of the generations in your workplace?

Minimal Monetary Methods for Motivating Millennials

Motivating employees doesn't have to bust your organization's budget. Here's a collection of low-cost or no-cost options for motivating and rewarding Millennials. Remember, seeing the value in these ideas—and actually remembering to do them—may require that you look through the lens of another generation's preferences, but you'll find quick success in connecting with the Millennials in your organization.

- Call and say thanks. Text the team acknowledging the Millennial's good work.

- Clip or forward magazine articles that remind you of them or their work style and write a note saying, "This strikes me as something you'd be up to trying. Would you like to work on this?"

- Create an internal web page for noting all the things people are doing right. Let everyone have access to add compliments.

- Find out the employee's hobbies and send interesting articles, links, or small gift cards for things related to the outside interest.

- Find out where they're going on vacation and send them links to your favorite restaurants (or their favorite type of restaurant) in that location.

- Give a small piggy bank full of pennies with a note saying, "If I had a penny for every time I hear something good about you, I'd have a heck of a lot more than this. Thanks for your hard work!"

- Give them a good book you've just finished and tell them why you thought they might be interested in it—or offer to purchase a favorite podcast for them.

- Give them a new challenge by assigning them a bigger role on a project.

- If the employee is featured on your intranet or company newsletter, send the link to the employee and suggest he/she forward it to his or her parents/friends.

- Keep a prize bucket with little toys from the party aisle at department stores. Have a prize day just because it's Monday.

- Keep a traveling trophy for excellence. Let the Millennial add his/her touch to the trophy when it's earned. Millennials from my sessions have suggested individual and unique plaques that mark their individualism.

- Pay for their lunch or coffee/soda/high energy drink in the cafeteria. For fun, do it anonymously and have the cafeteria clerk tell them that someone wanted to say thanks for their good work.

- Bring treats for the breakroom. One company I know of has Intern Thursday. The interns take pizza orders from regular employees, then bake the pizza in the company stove. They like it because they meet people from across the company.

- Send a text message to the team acknowledging her/his good work.

- Send the employee home an hour early with pay or tell the employee to come in an hour late with pay.

- Allow them to attend a class/training they are interested in.

Supporting Generations through Conflict and Change

Conflict and change can be challenging for anyone. Individually, each of us has a particular degree of risk tolerance that influences how we deal with these inevitable aspects of life. Our generational perspective also has an impact on our attitudes and behaviors through challenging times.

For a quick overview of how each generation deals with conflict and change, see Table 5 on page 38. Consider how closely you follow your generational profile in these areas. Can you see how you might need to stretch to support other generations?

 TALK TO ME: *My friend Mandi returned to work at a large corporation after several years as an independent consultant. After only a few months back in the corporate world, she was blindsided after completing a major divisional project. The hang-up? She hadn't talked to all the right people— and those right people complained to the VP. When her manager scolded her, Mandi (an Xer like me) defended her actions, cursed corporate inefficiency for holding her back, and refused to play what she saw as the corporate "game." As a result, her project was shelved. Later, a Boomer, more adept at talking through the conflicting sides of corporate politics, reinvented her project and received rave reviews from the division.*

TOOLS FOR REAL LIFE: *What types of conflict do you need to address with your team? What generational approaches might you use to support your team when conflict arises?*

Acknowledging Endings

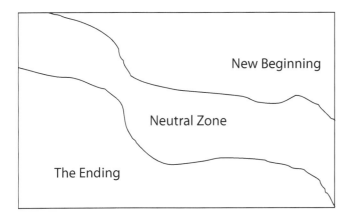

I thank William Bridges and Associates for permission to use this simple model to provide a deeper understanding of our different responses to change. Bridges suggests that in periods of change we travel from what we know (the ending) across a time of uncertainty (the neutral zone) to the new process or idea (new beginning). This trip through change is different for each person—and each generation.

As we leave the ending, we mourn what we're losing—and what we perceive as a loss differs according to our generational perspective. For example, when we ask a person from the WWII generation to text clients instead of making face-to-face visits, we're asking that person to give up a key generational value—loyalty to a process that has worked well for them.

Table 5: Supporting the Generations through Conflict and Change

	WORLD WAR II	BABY BOOM
Approximate birth years	• 1925 to 1945	• 1946 to 1964
About conflict...	• I follow orders, no questions asked, and so should you • Keep your conflict to yourself, it's none of my business	• I take on the issues I don't agree with, but believe conflict is dealt with best by resolving it as a team
Attitude toward conflict and other generations	• Other generations should agree with the chain of command or address conflict in a professional, behind-closed-doors way	• Conflict can be resolved with enough communication
What they'd tell other generations	• Buck up and deal with what you've been given. • I don't appreciate an attitude of "I deserve this" or "I learned this in school, it must be true."	• I resent you coming in and offering expertise that surpasses my knowledge. You're making me look bad. • I also don't appreciate the Lone Ranger approach. Ask me. I'll help if you ask.
What they give up during a change	• Loyalty • Security of knowing place in chain of command	• Status • Prestige • Competitive edge
How to support them through change	• Realize you are asking them to leave something they are loyal to • Give them time to adjust • Ask for their experience in this change	• Recognize that when you introduce change into their workplace, you are threatening to take away their competitive advantage and status • Assure them that you've talked to the right people (meaning them) and gained consensus about the change taking place

GENERATION X	MILLENNIAL
• 1965 to 1982	• 1982 to 2000
• I call it like I see it, even if it's not popular ~or~ I don't really care; this is my job; I'm here to do my job and go home	• I don't know what to do, so I avoid face-to-face conflict, especially when it comes to customer service
• Will ask why and question everything; are blindsided by corporate politics that result when too honest	• Assume the generations can get along with one another; resent conflict caused by Gen X brashness or Boomers' take-it-on conflict style (although appreciate Boomers' team resolution)
• If you don't like what you see or hear, stop whining and move on. • Just because I don't follow office politics doesn't mean I don't care. I'm tired of people gossiping and not doing their jobs. Who has time for that? I need to get home!	• I'm young, but I have good ideas. • Even when my ideas seem different, I'd appreciate help understanding why they are good or need improvement. • Don't tell me it hasn't worked before.
• Independence • Flexibility • Transparency	• Close-knit friendships
• Recognize the loss of independence and flexibility • Find ways to compensate by offering options, comp time, practical rewards and thank yous for extra time put in • Be transparent through the change. Closed doors are really annoying to this group—they've already assumed the worst, so just tell them what's going on	• Expect them to embrace new ideas fluidly, but help them understand why their suggestions for change may be so threatening to other generations

It can be extremely useful to recognize that when we are asking an individual to change, we may be asking that person to give up something of importance to her or his generation. Acknowledging these losses can be important. See Table 5 for more suggestions about how to support the generations through change.

 TALK TO ME: *Not too long ago, my church converted the old gymnasium into a video café. There was a lot of protest, from a lot of generations. When the ministry leadership team contemplated what they could have done differently, they were clear that they could have communicated the intent of the new space and venue to everyone. From a generational perspective, they came up with specific approaches that would have helped:*

- *Communicate to members of the WWII generation that their sacrifice is appreciated by other generations. Make it clear that they'll be given a different space and are not simply being ousted because they're no longer needed or appreciated.*

- *Help Boomers transition by getting more input and achieving consensus about what's happening.*

- *Explain the reason for the change to Xers, who value transparency. Surprisingly, Xers were the ones leaders thought would attend the service in this setting, but the Xers were oblivious to that perception because no one mentioned the intention to them.*

- *Engage Millennials in designing the new space and include them in developing the service. In this case, Millennials thought the whole space would be their cool hangout. They didn't realize it was for everyone, leaving them feeling disenchanted when they had to adapt to other generations' ideas about the space.*

 TOOLS FOR REAL LIFE: *What changes do you need to introduce to your organization or family? What are the key losses each generation will face during the change? How can you minimize and/or acknowledge those losses?*

Resources

Top Picks

My top pick for a deeper look into who the generations are and why they are that way:

> *When Generations Collide.* L. Lancaster & D. Stillman, Harper Business, 2002.

> *M-Factor.* L. Lancaster & D. Stillman, Harper Business, 2010.

My favorite author on Millennial-specific topics:

> Eric Chester, founder of www.GenerationWhy.com

More terrific books

Bridging the Generation Gap. Gravett, L. & Throckmorton, R., Book-mart Press, 2007.

Employing Generation Why? E. Chester, Tucker House Books, 2002.

Generation Me. J. Twenge, Free Press, 2006.

Getting Them to Give a Damn: How to Get Your Front Line to Care About Your Bottom Line. E. Chester, Kaplan Publishing, 2005.

Managing Generation Y. C. Martin, HRD Press, 2001.

Managing the Generation Mix. C. Martin & B. Tulgan, HRD Press, 2002.

Millennial Leaders: Success Stories from Today's Most Brilliant Generation Y Leaders. B. Fields, S. Wilder, J. Bunch & R. Newbold, Round Table Press, 2008.

Transitions: Making Sense of Life's Changes. Revised 25th Anniversary Edition. W. Bridges, Da Capo Press, 2004.

43672212R00032

Made in the USA
San Bernardino, CA
22 December 2016